MONARCH BUTTERFLIES

by Laura Hamilton Waxman

Lerner Publications Company • Minneapolis

This book is available in two editions:
Library binding by Lerner Publications Company, a division of Lerner Publishing Group
Soft cover by First Avenue Editions, an imprint of Lerner Publishing Group
241 First Avenue North
Minneapolis, MN 55401

Website address: www.lernerbooks.com

Words in *italic* type are explained in a glossary on page 30.

Library of Congress Cataloging-in-Publication Data

Waxman, Laura Hamilton.
    Monarch butterflies / by Laura Hamilton Waxman.
        p.   cm. — (Pull ahead books)
    Summary: Describes the stages of the life cycle of
the monarch butterfly.
    ISBN: 0–8225–4669–8 (lib. bdg. : alk. paper)
    ISBN: 0–8225–3647–1 (pbk. : alk. paper)
    1. Monarch butterfly—Juvenile literature.
[1. Monarch butterfly. 2. Butterflies.] I. Title. II. Series.
QL561.D3 W39 2003
595.78'9—dc21   2002009860

Manufactured in the United States of America
1 2 3 4 5 6 — JR — 08 07 06 05 04 03

Swish! A colorful butterfly flutters its wings.

What kind of butterfly is it?

This is a monarch butterfly.

A monarch butterfly is an *insect*.

Most insects have four wings.

A monarch's wings are orange,
black, and white.

Take a closer look at these wings.
Do you see the scales?

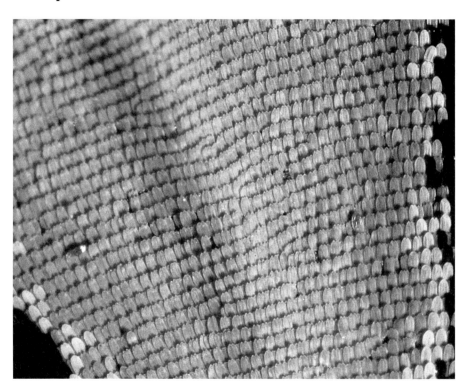

The scales protect monarchs
from rain.

A monarch uses its wings
to fly from flower to flower.

It uses its legs
to grab on to
flowers.

Inside each flower is a sweet juice.
The juice is called *nectar.*

A monarch butterfly sucks up the
nectar with its long black tongue.

A monarch finds new flowers
with the *two* *antennas* on its head.

Antennas help a monarch
feel and smell.

In the fall, flowers die. The weather becomes too cold for monarchs.

Many monarch butterflies
fly south to warm Mexico.

The traveling monarchs
sleep at night.

They hang
from bushes
and trees.

Hundreds of monarchs cling
to the trunk of this tree.

They have finally arrived in Mexico.
They will rest like this all winter.

When spring comes,
the monarchs return to the north.

What else happens in spring?

Spring is the time to begin
laying eggs.

Female monarchs lay their eggs
under leaves of milkweed plants.

Each egg is tiny and sticky.
It stays stuck to its leaf.

Look! Something is popping
its head out of this egg.

What is it?

It is a monarch *larva*.

Butterfly larvas are also called caterpillars.

Monarch larvas grow bigger each day. They eat and eat.

The larvas eat nothing but milkweed leaves.

A larva moves from one part
of the milkweed to another.

It uses its legs to move and
to hold on to the plant.

The larva keeps growing.
Its skin becomes too tight.

What will it do?

The larva *molts*.
It wiggles out of its tight skin.

Underneath is a new, bigger skin.
Can you find the old skin?

A larva stops eating and growing after about three weeks.

Then it finds a sturdy branch or twig to hang from.

The larva molts one last time.

It is becoming a *chrysalis*.

Something amazing is happening to the chrysalis.

Can you guess what it is?

The chrysalis is becoming a monarch butterfly!

Out comes the butterfly.
Its wings are soft and wet.

Soon the
wings will
harden
and dry.

This new monarch is ready to fly!

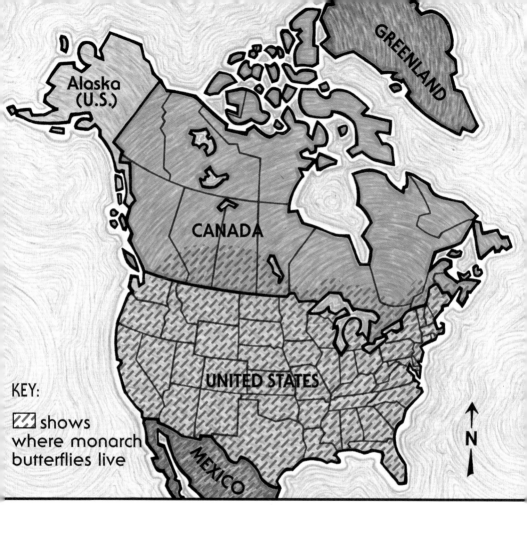

KEY:

shows where monarch butterflies live

Find your state or province on this map.
Do monarch butterflies live near you?

Parts of a Monarch Butterfly

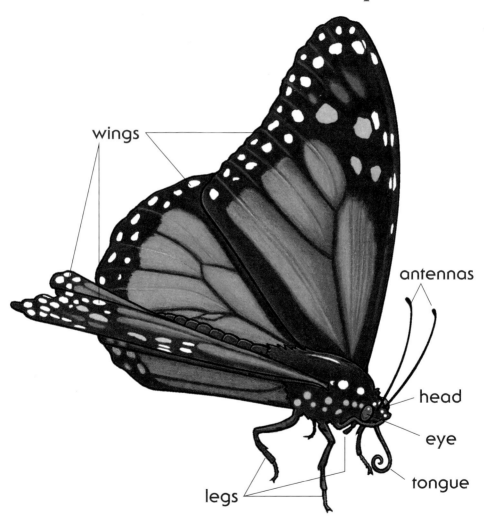

wings

antennas

head

eye

tongue

legs

Glossary

antennas: the feelers on a butterfly's head

chrysalis: the stage in a butterfly's life after it is a larva and before it is an adult. A chrysalis is covered by a hard outer shell.

insect: a small animal that has three main body parts and six legs. Most insects have four wings.

larva: a butterfly just after it has hatched from its egg. Butterfly larvas are also called caterpillars.

molts: gets rid of an old, tight skin

nectar: the sweet juice found in flowers